PETERBOROUGH
THEN and NOW

A Portrait in Photographs and Old Picture Postcards

by

June and Vernon Bull and Rita McKenzie

S. B. Publications

1992

First published in 1992 by S. B. Publications

Unit 2, The Old Station Yard, Pipe Gate,
Market Drayton, Shropshire TF9 4HY.

© Copyright 1992 June and Vernon Bull and Rita McKenzie

All rights reserved

ISBN 1 85770 022 8

Typeset and printed by Geo. R. Reeve Ltd., Wymondham, Norfolk NR18 0BD.

CONTENTS

	page		page
Introduction	v	Broadway — The Hippodrome/Tesco	26-27
Bibliography and Acknowledgements	vi	Broadway — Skating Rink/Tesco	28-29
Market Place & Cathedral — Then and Now	1	Broadway	30-31
Church Street, Werrington	2-3	Long Causeway	32-33
Gunthorpe Road	4-5	Long Causeway	34-35
Walton Road/Lincoln Road	6-7	Market Place/Cathedral Square	36-37
Frederick Sage's Works/Precision Components Ltd	8-9	Market Place/Cathedral Square	38-39
Paul Pry Inn, Walton	10-11	St. Nicholas' Gateway	40-41
New England	12-13	Peterborough Cathedral Choir	42-43
303-305, Lincoln Road	14-15	Narrow Street/Bridge Street	44-45
The Tithe Barn/Elwes Hall, Church Walk	16-17	Broad Bridge Street/Bridge Street	46-47
Russell Street	18-19	Bishops Road	48-49
King's School	20-21	The Swimming Pool/The Lido	50-51
Broadway	22-23	Broad Bridge Street/Rivergate	52-53
Broadway	24-25	Broad Bridge Street/Bridge Street	54-55

CONTENTS

	page		page
River Nene	56-57	Cathedral	82-83
New Bridge	58-59	Westgate	84-85
View from the River Nene	60-61	Park Road Co-op/Westgate House	86-87
Peterborough United Football Club	62-63	Westgate	88-89
Stanground	64-65	Star Road	90-91
Orton Waterville	66-67	Eastfield Road	92-93
War Memorial Hospital/District Hospital	68-69	Dogsthorpe	94-95
G.N. Railway Station/B.R. Station	70-71	Cowgate	96-97
Crescent Bridge	72-73	Cowgate	98-99
North Station	74-75	Church Street	100-101
Westfield Road	76-77	Cumbergate	102-103
Westgate	78-79	Aerial View	104-105
Westgate	80-81	S.B. Publications	106

Front Cover: Peterborough Market Place and Cathedral   *Title Page:* Peterborough Cathedral

INTRODUCTION

Many people have suggested that we produce a book of Peterborough's past and present following the success of the series of publications, Peterborough: A Portrait in Old Picture Postcards. We decided to meet with this sole aim in mind. We have endeavoured to take you on a journey around this city, which once bore the name of Medeshamstede ('the dwelling in the meadow'), then Gildenburgh, Peter's Burgh and now Peterborough.

The first of our journeys begins by entering Peterborough through the villages of Werrington, Gunthorpe and Walton. Travelling along Lincoln Road in a southerly direction we pass through the city centre, over the river bridge, deviating into Stanground, before leaving via Orton Waterville.

Our second venture takes us from the west to the east of the city, taking in the railways, Baker Perkins, and the shopping streets of Westgate and Park Road.

Our outing finally ends with a walk down Cowgate into Church Street, with a view of the city from above!

Cowgate reminds us that in the middle of the nineteenth century trade was chiefly in cattle. In addition, commodities like corn, malt, coal and timber were prevalent until the late 1800s when the railways attracted mechanics and other skilled labour. Also, the brickyards caused an influx of general labourers. Today the city attracts commerce and light industry. The future looks bright, with the possibility of a Euro Rail link terminus to the rest of Europe being built. The city itself is currently expanding faster with population growth being greater than anywhere else in East Anglia. Peterborough people can well afford to be proud and posh — having once had an Earl of Peterborough, the last being Charles Mordaunt, who died in 1735; whilst the Peterborough and Fletton United Football Club colours were claret and gold, hence Peterborough United Football Club today is still 'The Posh' — albeit the colours are now blue and white.

Our pleasure and involvement as local historians has enabled us to work with enthusiasm. We trust this book will provide as much pleasure and invoke happy memories for new as well as older residents of Peterborough. This city's visual heritage must not be forgotten.

June & Vernon Bull
Rita McKenzie
October 1991

BIBLIOGRAPHY

G.D. Austin (1978)	*Peterborough Trams,* Greater Peterborough Arts Council
Judy Bunten and Alfred Savage	*Werrington Through the Ages*
Joy Cowland	*The Story of Walton*
Michael Gibson	*Aviation in Northamptonshire*
W.D. Larrett MA	*A History of The Kings School Peterborough,* Harrison & Sons Ltd
T.P. Nutt	*When Boongate was Bungate*
H.F. Tebbs	*How the City has Changed*
H.F. Tebbs	*Peterborough,* The Oleander Press
Peter Waszak	*Rail Centres — Peterborough,* Ian Allan Ltd
Leslie Webb	*Some Peterborough Buildings*
Wm.J. Willcock	*Walks and Rides In and Around Peterborough*
	Peterborough Advertiser, weekly periodical, on 35mm film, Peterborough Central Library

ACKNOWLEDGEMENTS

All 1991 photographs by Vernon Bull and David Burling.
The authors are indebted to the following people without whose help this book would not have been possible:

Mr A. Arlow
Cecil Baldwin
Molly Heard
Richard Hillier
Mildred Julyan
Neil Mitchell
Stephen Perry for additional editing
Chris & Carol Talbot
The late Messrs Harry Miles and John Gaunt
Photograph on page 52 (Bull & Dolphin) by kind permission of Reg Wilcox, Minster Photography
Photograph on page 74 (North Station) by kind permission of Douglas Thompson
Photograph on page 102 (Cumbergate) by kind permission of Peterborough City Council Museum & Art Gallery
Steve Benz for marketing
Frank Rhodes of Lightwood for editing and proof-reading.

MARKET PLACE & CATHEDRAL – 1920   **MARKET PLACE & CATHEDRAL – 1991**

CHURCH STREET, WERRINGTON, 1952

Church Street, originally called Town Street, looking from the Church towards The Green compares well to today's busy traffic scene. The Three Horse Shoes public house can be seen on the immediate right on both pictures. Notable inhabitants of the village of Werrington since 1766 to the present day include the families of Griffin, Lynn, Hardy and Sergeant. The pub is believed to date back to the early-eighteenth century, and in 1871 the owner was Mr. Thomas Lynn. The little green beside the pub used to lead to a row of cottages built in the 1700s, and beside these cottages was a lane that led to cherry orchards where the famous Werrington 'White Heart' and 'Black Heart' cherries were grown.

CHURCH STREET, WERRINGTON, 1991

Amberley Slope is where the cottages used to stand and can be seen on the right beyond The Three Horse Shoes pub. The pub is believed to have got its name from a once-adjoining smithy, owned by a Mr. Joseph Lynn. Later the blacksmith part moved over the road to where 'Kiddicare' is now. The road on the left is Pipistrelle Court, named after bats that frequented this area.

FLOODS, GUNTHORPE ROAD, 1912

How completely rural this photograph of Gunthorpe Road looks. It was taken during the week of storms, beginning 26 August 1912. Orchards existed along this stretch of road and it was a favourite area for 'scrumping'. The bridge was originally one of the boundaries of Werrington, and the spring which runs under the bridge is called Werrington Brook.

GUNTHORPE ROAD, 1991

Now it is much more urbanised, with houses and roads having been built. On the left is the junction of Lowther Gardens with Gunthorpe Road. Brookside Methodist Chapel can be seen on the right. Lowther Gardens was built between 1964 and 1967. The bridge and brook still remain.

WALTON TRAM TERMINUS, 1909

Peterborough Electric Traction Company replaced the horse-drawn buses with electric trams in January 1903. Tracks were laid to Walton, Dogsthorpe and Newark. There were 12 trams to begin with, later increasing to 14. Trams existed for 27 years and were at their busiest at the time of the Peterborough Show, held at Millfield. Frequent journeys were made from Long Causeway to the showground. The tram terminus in Walton was situated in Walton Road, now part of Lincoln Road. The tram in this photograph is on its way back to Market Place from Walton Terminus. At Walton the mission room was purchased by the Tram Company for the benefit of passengers as a waiting room, and used to stand on the left of the tram. Electricity was introduced to Walton directly from the Tramway system, and could only be used during tramway running hours.

LINCOLN ROAD, 1991

Very little remains today. The Royal Oak, just out of shot on the left of the Edwardian scene, built in 1849, no longer stands, and the present Royal Oak was rebuilt between 1935 and 1936. The road today is an integral part of Peterborough's road system. The once narrow track road has become a dual-carriageway, the A15.

FREDERICK SAGE'S WORKS, WALTON, 1914

Built by Frederick Sage & Co. Ltd. in 1911, next door to Peter Brotherhoods, as a shopfitters and hardwood joiners, the firm made twelve Short 184 seaplanes for the Admiralty during the first world war. They also made around 600 examples of the much-used Avro 504 K at their Walton works. When completed the machines were wheeled across the railway tracks and flown off from the now defunct nine-hole Walton Golf Links. In 1935 the business was transferred to South America, and in 1936 the site was purchased by the Aeronautical Corporation of Great Britain.

PRECISION COMPONENTS LTD., 1991

After only a year's trading, AERONCA, as it was known, went into liquidation and once again the works were closed. During the last war the factory in Windsor Avenue was used as an ordnance sub-depot and traces of the camouflage paint can still be seen on the walls of the factory now occupied by Precision Components Ltd. As our view from the railway line shows, the same disused water tower still stands to remind us of the original Sage factory, the name being perpetuated in Sage's Lane at Walton.

PAUL PRY INN, WALTON, 1936

The old Paul Pry Inn on the Lincoln Road at Walton originally stood nearer the road, with its frontage right up to the pavement and the main entrance on the side of the building. In the mid-1890s the licensee was Henry Bailey, whose other occupation was listed as vermin destroyer! The inn was demolished in 1936 and two shops, 'Premier Engraving' and 'Bette's Hair Stylists', now stand on the site.

PAUL PRY INN, WALTON, 1991

Now a Berni Inn licensed restaurant, the new Paul Pry, built in 1936, stands further back from the road and just to the south of the old inn. It stands near the site of the old Walton Bowling Green and Pleasure Grounds, which ran from east to west and is now part of the pub's play area for children. At one time there was a door in the front of the building, now replaced by a window. In addition the front door has been widened and a wrought iron balcony added above it.

NEW ENGLAND, early-1900s

Built by John Thompson, the Peterborough builder, at a cost of £300, this fountain was presented to the parishioners of New England in 1884 by Rev. C.R. Ball and his sisters in memory of their parents, Rebecca and Joseph Ball. It was unveiled at 1.30 p.m. on Thursday 6 November 1884, in the presence of Mayor William Barford, J.P. and the Corporation, following the laying of the foundation stone of King's School in Park Road at 11.45 a.m. on the same day.

NEW ENGLAND, 1991

Looking towards Walton at the junction of Lincoln Road and Bourges Boulevard, this area is known locally as the Triangle. The fountain is still preserved, but no longer in working order, and iron railings have replaced the posts and chain links. On the 31 May 1929 a bus shelter, complete with clock tower, was erected near the fountain at a cost of £400. No longer a meeting place for young and old, it stands like an island in a sea of busy traffic.

LEONARD STEBBINGS, CONFECTIONER & FRUITERER, 1939

This shop front is 303-305 Lincoln Road, and was a very popular shop for chocolates, toffees, fruits, home-made ice-cream and tobacco. How lovely the window display looks with its reminder of apples for health, oranges for beauty, and eat more fruit to keep fit. The shop itself was owned by Mr. Herbert, who rented it to Len & Kit Stebbings, who lived above the premises. To the right of Stebbings is Allen's, the butchers. Stebbings was a greengrocers on one side and a tobacconists on the other. One of the Saturday girls in the tobacconists was Miss Patricia Hird.

CO-OPERATIVE PHARMACY, 1991

After Mr. Stebbings, once a member of the Auxiliary Fire Service, retired with his wife, the premises had a number of uses. These included a grocer's shop, discount shop and finally, in 1989, the Co-op pharmacy moved from the corner of Alma Road to 303-307 Lincoln Road. The first floor was removed during alterations, whilst the ground floor was extended into the garden at the rear.

THE TITHE BARN, 1890

Two large barns once stood between Manor House Street and Church Walk. This 1918 sketch of the smaller of the barns, erected in the early 1300s, stands on the site of Elwes Hall, Church Walk, and was built by Abbot Adam of Boothby, completely of oak with stone rubble walls. It survived the Reformation and the Civil War. In 1890 it was bought by James McCullum Craig for £725. The stone walls were dismantled in 1892 leaving the timber framework standing until 1899. Some of the stonework from the barn was used to construct Rothesay Villas in Lincoln Road, between 1892 and 1893.

ELWES HALL, CHURCH WALK, 1991

The site of the smaller barn is where the Elwes Hall premises in Church Walk stand. This hall was built in 1934 and named Elwes Hall in memory of Rev. Dudley Cary Elwes, Rector of All Souls, 1910-1921, then Bishop of the Roman Catholic Diocese of Northampton. It was bought by Frank Perkins in 1967 as their social club; then refurbished in the 1980s to become a night-club, and bought in 1984 by 'Videotec', which provided a range of beer and cocktail bars to entertain the over-25s. Today the premises are empty and for sale.

RUSSELL STREET, 1907

Looking down Russell Street towards Lincoln Road the spire of All Souls Church can just be seen behind the Rechabite and Temperance Hall, which was built in 1873 and extended in 1882. The firm of Whittle, Cabinet Makers, of 56 Russell Street had their premises on the left of our picture, eventually moving the business to Park Road. The Freehold Land Society bought up blocks of land in this area and divided it into building plots. Whoever bought the plots built these terraced houses for railway workers with a general pattern of 'streets', the name being synonymous with rows of workers cottages. Russell Street may have taken its name from Lord Russell, the Whig Prime Minister in 1846-52 who was a close colleague of Sir Robert Heron, one of the City's M.P.s.

RUSSELL STREET, 1991

The Rechabite Hall, now modernised, still stands sentinel at the bottom of the street. It was once the home of the Salvation Army when they first came to Peterborough and now houses the A.U.E.W. When the A.U.E.W. took the hall over the deeds included a covenant still in force that forbids alcohol being consumed on the premises. The gap between the houses on the left has now been filled by a new extension and the railings on the right are replaced by a car entrance. Notice all the 'improved' house frontages.

CHEMISTRY LABORATORY, KING'S SCHOOL, PARK ROAD, c.1944
The whole science block was built in 1912, financed by the generosity of Walter Ernest Cross, Headmaster, and former Senior Science Master of Whitgift School, Croydon. Cross later resigned his headship in 1913 to become headmaster of Maidstone Grammar School. He had done much to enhance the sciences at King's School, using his own money!

METALWORK ROOM, KING'S SCHOOL, 1991
No longer used as a chemistry laboratory but a metalwork room. Pupils pictured today include Robert Newlyn, Richard Flatters, Gareth Jones with technician Brian Shearsmith in the background.

BROADWAY, SHOWING PUBLIC LIBRARY, 1957

The old public library building on the left of the picture was opened by Mr. Andrew Carnegie; the famous Scottish-American millionaire and first Freeman of the City of Peterborough. The old library building comprising reference room, junior and adult rooms. The Theatre Royal in the backgound was built in 1877 with its main entrance facing Park Road; architects Pye and Hayward of London originally built the premises as an indoor skating rink, and public hall (namely the Fitzwilliam Hall). In April 1916 it briefly changed its name to The Grand. It finally closed as the Theatre Royal and Empire in 1957. Now Sheltons Department Store stands on the site.

BROADWAY, 1991

Broadway is quite different today; only the library (opened in 1905 and closed to the public in 1990) remains the same in both pictures. Sheltons department store occupies the site of the Theatre Royal and Empire, and is presently being redeveloped for other use. The old library building is being refurbished to become the city's newest and most exciting nightclub. Fairways site is now the new public library, officially opened by the Duke of Gloucester in 1991. On the corner of Cattle Market Road, where Emways Garage was situated, is the new prestigious office block called Bayard Place.

BROADWAY, early-1900s

The Peterborough Cattle Market Co., was formed in May 1863, built partly on a field called Simpsons Place. The land had been bought from Earl Fitzwilliam in 1861. After being held in Long Causeway for many years prior to this, it finally opened on the 17 February 1866, with Mr. Robert Wright as the first Cattle Market superintendent. In 1891 the Corporation bought the Cattle Market rights from the P.C.M.C. and it finally closed in the spring of 1972.

Peterborough's general market was relocated there in 1963 and still remains to carry on the old market traditions.

BROADWAY, 1991

This view is from the window of the new Central Library, built on the site of Fairways store and opened in 1990, whereas the previous photo was taken a few yards further south, from the window of the old library which had first opened on 4 December 1905. On the right the Cannon Cinema, previously the Embassy theatre, was opened in 1937 and now stands empty at the entrance to Cattle Market Road. Finally, to obliterate the scheme entirely, we now see under construction the imposing five-storey office building called Bayard Place, situated at the corner of Broadway and Northminster.

THE HIPPODROME, BROADWAY, 1912

In 1908 the Hippodrome was bought by the famous theatrical troupe owner, Fred Karno. Many great comedians worked for Karno: Max Miller, Charlie Chaplin, Sandy Powell, and Flanagan and Allen. In 1924 the Bancroft family took a lease on the Hippodrome, located in Broadway, on the site now occupied by Tesco's Supermarket. In 1930 the Bancrofts eventually purchased the Hippodrome, by then renamed The Palace, and by 1937 they built the Embassy Cinema as The Palace was too small and rather primitive. Here, in this 1912 postcard, Edie and Fay Black appear as a singing and dancing duet.

TESCO SUPERMARKET, BROADWAY, 1991
Here is the entrance to Tesco's Supermarket in Broadway, one of Britain's top ten Supermarket chains. Tesco display enlarged old photographs and picture postcards in their store so our local visual heritage is not forgotten.

BROADWAY, 1911

Situated opposite the old Broadway Electric Theatre and next door to the Hippodrome, built two years previously, was the Peterborough Pavilion Roller Skating Rink. Opened on the 8 December 1909 and with uniformed commissionaire outside, it had a fairly short-lived life as in 1913-14 it was closed and converted into Brainsby's motor repair garage. At the same time there was another skating rink in Westgate called 'The Princess', so perhaps this proved to be the more popular venue of the two.

TESCO, BROADWAY, 1991
The first phase of Tesco's popular supermarket opened in the mid-1960s and was built as part of the Hereward Shopping Centre (now known as Hereward Cross). Mann Egerton (Johnson) Ltd. bought Reeds garage, formerly Brainsby's, on Broadway in 1961 and dealt in Morris, MG, Riley and Wolseley cars. They ceased trading at the end of January 1978 and this building was demolished for Tesco's extension, erected in 1981. The Pavilion skating rink was exactly where Mann Egertons garage used to be.

BROADWAY, 1918

This parade of discharged sailors and soldiers took place on 21 September 1918. Notice The Hippodrome theatre on the right and The Theatre Royal, centre left, which was an indoor skating rink before Peterborough Pavilion Roller-Skating Rink was built adjacent to The Hippodrome. The City Surveyor's Office is located in the right foreground, whilst top left is the Broadway Kinema, formerly the Broadway Electric Theatre, until it changed hands in 1913. The Broadway Electric Theatre was Peterborough's first picture house. The parade of soldiers and sailors started in Stanley Recreation Ground and the marchers proceeded to Market Place, then on to Cowgate, into St. Leonard's Street and finally gathered at Newtown National School, Nelson Street.

BROADWAY, 1991
A new office block now stands on the corner of Broadway and Cattle Market Road, whilst on the opposite corner is the redundant Embassy Cinema building, latterly owned by Cannon Cinemas. Sheltons store now occupies the site of The Theatre Royal and Empire.

LONG CAUSEWAY, PETERBORO'

LONG CAUSEWAY, 1915

This busy scene shows a varied mixture of old vehicles including two different styles of perambulator and assorted hand carts and wagons, one of them belonging to Paten and Co., wine & spirit merchants in Long Causeway. Taken at the crossroads with Broadway, Westgate and Midgate, Thomas L. Barrett's corner drapery store known as 'Waterloo House' can be seen on the left. When the foundations were dug for this large store in January 1884 the original deep town drain was uncovered, being three feet wide and giving the appearance of a bed of black mud!

LONG CAUSEWAY, 1991

No flower-bedecked lamp and tram posts in the road now. Instead we see the signs indicating a pedestrian zone. There are wider pavements on each side and trees obscure the distant view of the Midland Bank in the centre of our picture. Traces of the old buildings can still be seen on the right hand corner, but on the left the large modern buildings of Midgate House replace 'Barrett's Corner', demolished in 1974.

LONG CAUSEWAY, 1905

Looking down Long Causeway to Barrett's Corner, with a tram returning to the market. On the immediate left is Brainsby & Sons, leading carriage and wagon makers; Duddington's toy shop is on the corner of Cumbergate, with the Midland Counties District Bank on the opposite corner. Notice on the far right, just past the second tram, are the offices of Stones' mineral water manufacturers, spirit merchants and beer dealers, whose works were in Towler Street.

LONG CAUSEWAY, 1991
The whole of Cumbergate has been re-developed and forms part of the Queensgate Shopping Complex, officially opened by Queen Beatrix of the Netherlands in November 1982. Also Long Causeway is now pedestrianised, with trees flanking the pavements.

MARKET PLACE, 1905

A panoramic view of Market Place. The Abbey was granted the right to hold a market at Peterborough by King Edgar in AD972. From AD1200 market days were held on Wednesdays and Saturdays instead of Sundays. Everything from dairy produce to poultry, fruit and vegetables was sold in the square. By 1865 the butcher and farming interests moved into Cattle Market Road, and were dealing directly with Smithfield Market in London due to the direct rail link. However spinning, malting and the marketing of wild ducks from the Fens was popular until 1927.

CATHEDRAL SQUARE, 1991

In 1963 the general market was moved from Cathedral Square to where the old cattle market stood near New Road. By 1979 the new modernised fish and meat market, as we know it today, was opened, along with the first multi-storey car park, nearby. Today Cathedral Square is less busy as a Market Square except at Christmas, when amusement stalls and other entertainment promotions take place.

MARKET PLACE, 1913

Probably taken on 'Mayor's Sunday', when the City Brigade always formed the Mayor's escort. These firemen are marching proudly past the Market Place towards Cowgate. Leading them is the city's first Electrical Engineer and also first Chief Fire Officer, Captain John C. Gill. Boots Cash Chemists, at 8 Market Place, can be seen in the centre with its lovely pargetted plasterwork, completed in 1911 when this branch was built. The first Boots was opened in Narrow Bridge Street in 1894, followed by a second branch in Westgate in 1895.

CATHEDRAL SQUARE, 1991

The fondness of Jesse Boot and his wife for expensive Medieval and Tudor style shop fronts can still be seen, but a fast food shop replaces Boots Cash Chemists. These members of the Peterborough Volunteer Fire Brigade certainly lived up to their motto, 'Ready and Willing', by re-enacting our previous photograph. *Leader:* G.C. Sayers. *Near side (front to rear):* R.B. Rate, A. DeMatteis, P. Pearce, P.S. Ruff, L. Rumsey, K. Maxwell. *Far side (front to rear):* C.E. Cooke, P. Lloyd, B. Crutchfield, A.C. Pickering, T. Kelly, M. Connolly.

ST. NICHOLAS' GATEWAY, PETERBOROUGH CATHEDRAL, 1909

So called because the Chapel of St. Nicholas was above the archway, formerly used as part of the King's Grammar School and also as a library by the Peterborough Gentleman's Society. At this time Messrs. W. Boughton and Sons, artist and photographers, occupied the Cathedral Studio on the right of the St. Nicholas' Gateway leading to the Cathedral's West Front. On the left, J. Fairweather & Son, coal and coke merchants, had their offices. Peterborough's museum was located in St. Thomas A Becket Chapel, to the left after passing through the gateway. A sign advertising this fact can be seen on the right hand side of this Edwardian postcard.

ST. NICHOLAS' GATEWAY, 1991

Today the view shows Lloyds Bank, built 1913-1914, to the left of St. Nicholas' Gateway, with plastic benches replacing the Cathedral Studio site. The nave of St. Thomas A Becket's Chapel was demolished to make way for the bank. The Gate to the Archway was created by Abbot Benedict in the Norman Style. Part of the King's Lodgings on the right of the gate was at one time a gaol, the door of which was preserved in Peterborough Museum. The King's Lodgings, now unoccupied, has been a pharmacy as well as home to an Estate Agent in recent years.

41

PETERBOROUGH CATHEDRAL CHOIR, 1904

A local couplet runs, *'Peterborough Minster would not have been so high, if Barnack Quarry had not been so nigh'*. Taken near one of these high magnificent early-English arches of the West Front of Peterborough Cathedral, this postcard shows the choir of 1904. Two names written on the front are Phillips and Davidson, these being Dr Stephen Phillips, Minor Canon 1876-1883 and 1893-1906 (Precentor and Sacristan 1877-1883, Precentor 1893-1906) and Gerard Markby Davidson, Minor Canon 1901-1906 (Sacristan 1906). The Organist and Master of Choristers at the time was H. Keeton, Mus. Doc. Oxon.

PETERBOROUGH CATHEDRAL CHOIR, 1991

Although the Cathedral Choir is larger than shown here, the picture is taken in exactly the same place with an identical number of people. *Back row (left to right):* Jerome de Silva, Mark Newitt, Miles Allchurch, Gregory Sueling, Graeme Smith, Gareth Davies, Simon Newitt, Christopher Wearmouth. *Middle row (left to right):* Philip Krinks, Benjamin Carter, Alexander Phillips, Noel Reeves, Guy Plaistere, James Barber, Christopher Peters, Rhys Walsh, Jonathan Birley, Hugh Potton. *Front row (left to right):* Michael Riley, Simon Arnold, Canon Thomas Christie, Christopher Gower (Master of the Music), Andrew Plant, Peter Sproule.

NARROW STREET, PETERBOROUGH

NARROW STREET, 1927

Taken from Market Place (Cathedral Square). The north end of Narrow Street is pictured with the Midland Bank in the right foreground. Shops in Market Place include: in the left foreground, Caster & Jelley, booksellers and stationers; J.W. Williamson, toy shop; London Furnishings, removal contractors. Narrow Street begins with Pearson's, druggists, opposite the Midland; followed by T.C. Palmer, tailors; Currys Ltd., cycle store; J. Lefevre & Sons, saddlers; Hepworth & Sons, tailors; etc. On the right after the Midland Bank in Narrow Street is Masons Ltd., food provisions; G. Gaunt, outfitters; Madame Gray, milliner; J.W. Haylock Ltd., boot & shoe stores; etc.

BRIDGE STREET, 1991

The 1927 view is completely unrecognisable today, as Bridge Street was widened in the 1930s to facilitate the new municipal buildings finally completed in 1933. Narrow Street became incorporated into Bridge Street. Only the Midland Bank building remains as a reminder. It was one of the largest buildings of its time and caused great controversy when it was built in 1902, because the proposed widening of Narrow Street was to take place by utilising the site on which the bank was eventually built.

BROAD BRIDGE STREET, 1905

Looking north towards Narrow Bridge Street from Broad Bridge Street, Albert Place can just be seen on the left hand corner, now replaced by Bourges Boulevard. The Golden Lion Commercial Hotel, with its sign, 'Cyclists and tourists well catered for', ended its life as a garage. The building was demolished in 1927 and Narrow Street widened (being only 20 feet between the buildings on either side) to make way for the Town Hall and new shops on its east side. In 1931, Narrow Street disappeared for ever and was renamed simply Bridge Street.

BRIDGE STREET, 1991

Over eighty-five years have elapsed between these two photographs with the construction of Bourges Boulevard (named after our French twin town of Bourges) totally dividing the two parts of Bridge Street. Now, as then, it is still one of our main shopping and pedestrian thoroughfares, with Woolworths and Marks & Spencer on the left and the Town Hall and municipal buildings on the right. These are said to be based on a design for Chelsea Barracks.

BUS STATION, BISHOPS ROAD, 1953

A view of Peterborough's lively bus station, built at a cost of £3210, located opposite the outdoor swimming pool, The Lido, Bishops Road. The first double-decker buses were introduced in 1924 by Peterborough Electric Traction Company. In 1931 the Traction Company merged with the Eastern Counties Omnibus Company. At the time of this picture the company had a fleet of 77 buses covering routes totalling over 500 miles. They boasted that they had a monopoly on many routes, having bought out several local operators.

BISHOPS ROAD, 1991
Sadly, the Bishops Road site closed as a bus terminus in the early 1980s. The new bus station is incorporated into Queensgate indoor shopping complex, and the former bus station site is now occupied by Peterborough Crown Court.

A CORNER OF THE BATHING POOL, PETERBOROUGH.

THE SWIMMING POOL, 1937

The open air swimming pool situated in Bishops Road was built in 1936 to the design of a local panel of architects. The main pool is 165 feet by 60 feet, varying from 3 feet to 9 feet in depth. A standard 5 metre diving stage is also provided. The children's pool is 70 feet by 24 feet. In 6 hours the filtration plant is capable of treating the full capacity of the pools' water — all 388,000 gallons. Changing rooms and lockers are provided and a cafe serves both the terrace and bathing surrounds. The pools are illuminated under water and are open from May to September.

THE LIDO, 1991

Today the pool is called 'The Lido'. Just as many people use the outdoor pool as they ever did — despite the new heated indoor pool nearby. Recent moves by the City Council to close 'The Lido' have met with strong local resistance. Many people prefer the art deco design and insist that the old and new can co-exist. Certainly the only difference between today's view and yesteryear's is the lack of deck chairs on the terraces and sun loungers at ground level. Obviously the demolition of the fountain at the bottom end of the main pool takes some of the ambience away.

51

BROAD BRIDGE STREET, early 1900s

The Bull & Dolphin drinking saloon and wine store was occupied by Alfred John Paten, who bought it in 1898 from Alderman Nicholls, three times Mayor of Peterborough. The previous tenants were a Mr & Mrs White, and it was a house for tradesmen, where each customer had his own chair and churchwarden pipe, and woe betide the man who occupied another persons chair! Next door, to the right, was the family grocer Mr W. Bodger, father of the Museum curator Mr J. W. Bodger. The famous Bodger's treacle and firkin butter were sold at the shop.

RIVERGATE, 1991

Keeping in line with the restoration of buildings along this part of the Rivergate complex, Collyweston slates have been put on the roof of the old Bull & Dolphin pub, now Key Consultants Ltd. It is thought that this type of slate has not been used in Peterborough for over forty years. The pub belonged to the Paten family for seventy-five years, an unusual feature being that it served tea and coffee as well as alcohol. It closed in the early 1970s when it was sold to Ansells.

BROAD BRIDGE STREET, 1905

Originally held on 21-23 September, Bridge Fair was always an occasion for people to pour into the City, and in 1859 four railway companies brought 9,500 people to the Peterborough Fair. In 1905, this was not the last fair, as the postcard proclaims, but at the time there was much discussion amongst City Councillors, who proposed to do away with the opening ceremony. General opinion was that it had been deprived of the dignity it merited, council members looked like fools and the ceremony was not being conducted in a seemly manner!

BRIDGE STREET, 1991

Taken from the same windows of the old Temperance Hotel, now the empty building of 'Viva La Rock' next to the town bridge. Who could have foreseen the changes that have taken place here, with only the spires of the cathedral in the distance still the same? On the right can be seen the Bridge Street Police Station and the new road system filtering around the Magistrates court, opened by the Queen in 1978.

RIVER NENE FROM THE TOWN BRIDGE, 1924

This scene shows how far the river bank has been eroded. Also during Edwardian times you could hire a row-boat from the Custom House quay. The present Custom House building dates from the early-eighteenth century. Barges or Fen 'lighters' used to move up and down the River Nene with their cargoes of grain, stone, coal, and malt. Fees for river traffic continued up until as late as 1910, the Custom House monitoring the flow of cargo and collection of tolls. Goods shipped along the river were held here until the appropriate tolls were paid, and they would then be shipped upstream to Northampton or downstream to Wisbech.

RIVER NENE, 1991

An alternative to hiring a boat at the quayside is to enjoy a Chinese meal on board 'The Grain Barge' floating restaurant, which specialises in Szechuan and Cantonese dishes. The Custom House is now used by the Sea Cadets, being their headquarters since 1942. The City Council acquired the building in 1949 and the quay at the foot of Bridge Street is gone completely. During the Napoleonic wars French prisoners were brought by river to Peterborough, disembarked near the Custom House and marched to the prisoner-of-war camp at Norman Cross.

New Bridge, Peterborough

NEW BRIDGE, 1950

Dominating the skyline behind the imposing concrete bridge completed in 1934 are the chimneys of the Electricity Power Station. The 120 ft chimney on the right was built between 1925 and 1929, and the chimney on the left between 1948 and 1951. Notice that when this photograph was taken it was still called the 'New' bridge — sixteen years after it had been built. The first power station was originally to be built in Queen Street, but was eventually built on Albert Place Meadows, as it had the advantage of being adjacent to the River Nene and also the Great Northern Railway. The first business premises were supplied with electricity on the 19 December 1900, just in time for a brighter Christmas!

NEW BRIDGE, 1991

This picture of the bridge, now built for nearly sixty years, is taken from the same place at Bridge House's river frontage, on the south bank of the Nene. The final demolition of the Electric Power Station took place in 1979-80, and the tops of the Rivergate flats can just be seen behind the bridge, replacing the Patent Ladder Company's extensive works. The old Temperance Hotel still survives on the corner of the bridge, as does the Custom House on the right, now known as Training Ship *Gildenburgh,* the headquarters of the local Sea Cadet Corps., since 1942.

VIEW FROM THE RIVER NENE, 1908

Probably taken from the historic railway bridge built in 1850 over Wood Fair Meadow, we look east down the River Nene towards the town bridge when it was still an iron one. This shows the north side of the river bank, with its assortment of houses and businesses including the boat yard and the Patent Safety Ladder Co., at one time a timber yard occupied by John Hobbs. The only building still recognisable now is the Custom House, c.1700, on the far side of the bridge, all the other buildings having gone.

VIEW FROM THE RIVER NENE, 1991

Too dangerous now to take this photograph from the old railway bridge, so we have come a bit nearer to the north bank and taken it from the new footbridge. This area now looks very attractive with its development of new flats called 'Rivergate'. When first advertised for sale they were said to be the most expensive luxury flats ever offered for sale in Peterborough and were supposed to appeal to professional couples and London 'yuppies'!

PETERBOROUGH UNITED FOOTBALL CLUB, 1961

Peterborough United, known throughout the football world as 'The Posh', tried since 1942 to get into the Football League, but it was not until 1960, after scoring 108 goals and topping the Midland Counties League again, that they were accepted into the Fourth Division. In their first season they made history by topping the league table with 66 points, and scored 134 goals, more goals than any team had scored in any division at this time.

Back Row (left to right): R. Banham, C. Sansby, J. Anderson, J. Walls, J. Walker
Middle row (left to right): R. Whittaker, R. Jacobs, G. Graham, D. Emery, N. Rigby, D. Norris, J. Dunne, K. Ripley
Front Row (left to right): W. Hails, C. Coates, T. Bly, J. Rayner, R. Smith, P. McNamee, T. Atkins, J. Sheavills
Seated (left to right): E. Stafford, J. Taylor, R. Cooper.

PETERBOROUGH UNITED FOOTBALL CLUB, 1991

Still affectionately known as 'The Posh', the team is presently riding on a stream of good luck as they sweep into the third round of the Rumbelows League Cup by toppling First Division Wimbledon. This is only the third time in 13 years.
Back row (left to right): Mick Halsall, Garry Kimble, Garry Butterworth, Fred Barber, Kenny Charley, Micky Turner, Paul Culpin, Neil Pope.
Middle row (left to right): Bill Harvey (Club Physio.), Peter Costello, Chris Swailes, David Robinson, Ian Bennett, Steve Welsh, Pat Gavin, Hamish Curtis, Chris White, Keith Oaks (Team Physio.).
Front row (left to right): Marcus Ebdon, Ian McInerney, Worrell Sterling, Lil Fuccillo (Asst. Manager), Chris Turner (Manager), Gerry McElhinney (Youth Team Leader), Noel Luke, David Riley, Gary Cooper.

STANGROUND, 1922

The Chapel Street School at Stanground was completed 1st September 1900 and officially opened on 27 September 1900. The old school was closed and became the Parish Room. It had to be reopened in 1917, and again in 1922, when there were fires at the new school. The fire which took place on Thursday 15 June 1922 was quite severe and £2000 worth of damage was caused. Some painters had been at work using blowlamps for burning off old paint from the woodwork, and shortly after 6.15 pm it was noticed that the classroom at the north-east corner of the building was on fire. The firemen of the Fletton Fire Brigade were summoned, but a poor supply of water handicapped them considerably. The headmaster at the time was Mr A.W. Woodbridge.

STANGROUND, 1991

Taken at a different angle from our previous picture; the brick wall of the school bicycle sheds restrict the taking of the same view. Television aerials replace the cupola, a sign of the times in the classroom of today at St. John's Chapel Street Primary School. In 1922 it was known as the Council Mixed School, with accommodation for 270 children, and the average attendance was 180. A little girl called Ivy Elson was the first person to discover the fire. I wonder if she still remembers it today.

CHERRY ORTON ROAD, ORTON WATERVILLE, 1913

Looking towards Oundle Road. The London North Western Railway line used to service the 244 residents of Orton Waterville, with the station being a quarter of a mile away from the village. In 1913, principal residents of Orton Waterville, or Cherry Orton as it used to be known, included Albert Luke Claypole, a member of the Claypole family who traded from 55 Narrow Bridge Street, and Ganderton and Woodbridge, farmers.

ORTON WATERVILLE, 1991

Today the Windmill Pub, just out of shot to the right, still remains the same, as does this lovely thatched cottage. However, much of the open countryside has been developed to make way for houses.

Children's Ward, New War Memorial Hospital, Peterborough

WAR MEMORIAL HOSPITAL, 1929

Built as a memorial to the gallant dead of the first world war, The Peterborough Memorial Hospital, Midland Road, was opened by Field Marshal Sir William Robertson in June 1928. It was to be another year before the Children's Ward was completed. It was opened on 28 June 1929 by HRH Prince George, later the Duke of Kent. As a souvenir of the opening he was presented with an inscribed silver gilt key. The open plan sun parlour was at the end of the ward and was designed for the benefit of those children nearest to going home.

PETERBOROUGH DISTRICT HOSPITAL, 1991

With the growth of Peterborough as a new town it was felt a new hospital was needed, so in 1968 the old Memorial Hospital was closed down and the new District Hospital was opened, built by the Mitchell Construction Co. Then it was decided to turn the old hospital into a wing of the new one, necessitating many internal alterations. Part of the façade on the right has been altered, but the fire escape still remains, and the open plan sun parlour has had its external walls fitted with windows.

GREAT NORTHERN RAILWAY STATION, 1923-25
Peterborough North Station with the Great Northern Hotel on the right. A London North Western engine is at the head of the train in platform 1, whilst to the left a freight train is in motion on the Midland Line. This view is of the south end of the station. Spital Bridge locoshed can be seen in the left hand corner.

PETERBOROUGH RAILWAY STATION, 1991

Taken from Crescent Bridge the view today is completely changed. The locosheds have gone, and platform 1 is now used for trains carrying parcel post only. A speedy 125 train can be seen on platform 2. The footbridge that spans the tracks can be seen top of centre, and all the chimney stacks on the Great Northern Hotel have been levelled off.

OPENING OF CRESCENT BRIDGE, PETERBOROUGH APRIL 16 1913

CRESCENT BRIDGE, 1913

Crescent Bridge took its name from The Crescent, a row of thirteen Georgian terraced houses situated between Midland Road and Crescent Wharf. The site is now occupied by W.H. Smith and Sons Ltd., wholesale branch. These houses were demolished to build the new bridge over the railway, eventually replacing both a double level crossing and a subway. The bridge, costing £34,000 to build, was officially opened on 16 April 1913 by Mayoress J.G. Barford. Local dignitaries can be seen in procession walking down St. Leonards Street, previously called Common Muckhill.

NEAR CRESCENT BRIDGE, 1991

Adjacent to the Peterborough railway station is the entrance to a new multi-storey car park called 'Perkins', one of four operated by the Queensgate shopping centre and once part of St. Leonards Street. The other three car parks are 'Cavell', 'Royce' and 'Clare', all named after well-known local people in Peterborough's past. On the left can be seen part of the wall of the old railway buildings from our previous photograph, and, as before, the Great Northern Hotel, albeit modernised, is still in the background.

NORTH STATION, 1960s

This shows Peterborough's Great Northern railway station, opened in August 1850. Originally it was one of three stations in the city, the other two being Peterborough East station, demolished in 1972, and the L.M.S. station, only open for a short while from 1858-1866 and situated just south of Crescent Bridge. Looking north, a 9F 2-10-0 Freight Locomotive nicknamed *Spaceship* waits at the platform where once there was a separate waiting room for 'Ladies only'.

The covering roof has gone, there is a new footbridge, and even the old station clock has been replaced by a digital one.

PETERBOROUGH RAILWAY STATION, 1991

Apart from the Nene Valley Steam Railway, Peterborough North Station is now the only station in the city and is known as Peterborough Railway Station. There have been quite a few changes since our earlier photograph, the 'Intercity 125' train obviously being one of them. The new Travel Centre and passenger concourse was opened in July 1979 by Peterborough MP, Dr Brian Mawhinney, and the new station, costing £500,000, was opened in 1980 by the then chairman of British Rail, Sir Peter Parker.

WESTFIELD ROAD, 1933

Baker Perkins Ltd. was an amalgamation of a number of engineering firms, but mainly in 1919 of Perkins Engineers Ltd. and Joseph Baker & Sons Ltd. The firm abbreviated the names to Baker Perkins Ltd. in 1923, a year after the disastrous fire of March 1922, when the major part of the building was turned into a blackened ruin. There were works at Willesden, London and Westwood, Peterborough, but in 1933 the two came together under one roof at Peterborough and the new office building was erected. At the same time Willesden Avenue at Walton was built to house the workers who came to Peterborough from London. No. 5 Willesden Avenue was the showhouse for the company and was allocated to Mr Charles Bryant and his family.

WESTFIELD ROAD, 1991

This piece of road beyond Westwood Bridge had no name until after World War I, and was simply called Westfield. Baker Perkins, or 'Westwood Works' as it was fondly known, was acquired by A.P.V. plc in 1987 and the printing machinery company became known as A.P.V. Baker P.M.C. In March 1989 ownership passed to Rockwell International who acquired the business and the forty-two acre site in Westfield Road. A.P.V. Baker has moved to a new twenty-eight acre site at Manor Drive, Paston Parkway. Rockwell's is to close and the future of the old Baker Perkins factory site is yet to be decided.

WESTGATE, 1912

This was J.H. Smith's Umbrella Hospital, situated in Westgate between Wood Street and Milton Street, all of which has now gone to make way for Queensgate. Known as 'Postcard' Smith because of the large numbers of postcards he sold, he also had another shop at 12 Westgate, near the Bull Hotel. The hairdresser and tobacconist next door was Henry Howitt, and adjacent to him on the corner of Wood Street was the British Girls School. This was previously the Westgate Congregational Church, before it transferred to its present site across the road.

WESTGATE, 1991

Moving a few yards further along the road it is nice to see that some of the old buildings have been preserved; the Wortley Almshouses, now a public house, being one of them. This building, originally the workhouse, stood near the east corner of Wood Street and Westgate. In 1744 the house and land was given by the Hon. Edward Wortley Montagu 'for the better accommodation of the poor of St. John's parish'. Rebuilt in 1837 in Tudor style the house was then known as the Westgate Almshouses. In the background can be seen the high brick wall of the department store of the John Lewis Partnership.

WESTGATE, early 1900s

Lincoln Road, on the right, was originally a short cut known as Berygap, from Westgate to the stream which flowed from Craig Street to Park Road, and did not become a thoroughfare until the last century. The shop on the corner has had many different traders in its 200 year history including: an undertaker, a hat and bonnet maker, and one of the longest occupants — Thompsons the furniture makers. On the 21 February 1835 it escaped a disastrous fire which had begun in the present bus station area. This was mainly averted by the wine merchant who owned the 'Royal' hotel using his numerous carts and barrels to carry water to the fire. On the left can be seen the old 'Black Horse Inn', where one of the last licensees was Richard Stimson.

WESTGATE, 1991
Due for demolition to make way for more office development, this used to be a very busy newspaper shop, but is now the only building left standing on this corner. It had been a newsagents for many years, at one time run by three sisters by the name of Hubbard. Known as Johnsons Corner, it then had a run of 23 years, until 1973, under the ownership of Charles Ruckwood, who sold it to Mr Willey. The last owners, until it was vacated in 1989, were Plumbs the newsagents.

Peterborough Cathedral, Baptist Chapel and St. John's Church

CATHEDRAL, BAPTIST CHAPEL, ST. JOHN'S CHURCH, 1904

This view, looking north-west, depicts the Queen Street Baptist Chapel before the fire in 1905. The Rev. Henry Knee was pastor. Also, to the right is Peterborough's Parish Church of St. John the Baptist, which is built in the Perpendicular style and was founded in 1407. The Cathedral Church of St. Peter was originally the Church of the Abbey of St. Peter which, before the Reformation, lay within the Diocese of Lincoln. The Abbey was dissolved in 1539, and two years later the church became the cathedral, the spiritual 'head' of the newly-created Diocese of Peterborough.

CATHEDRAL, 1991

The 1904 view was probably taken from the roof of a building in Westgate, whilst the present view was taken from Baker Perkins office block in Westfield Road. As you can see, virtually all of Queen Street and all of Cumbergate, Milton Street, Wood Street and Deacon Street have disappeared under Queensgate shopping complex, which is the largest covered shopping area in the East Midlands. Built at a cost of nearly £30 million, it was opened to the public on 3 March 1982. A new bus station was constructed too, in Bourges Boulevard, opposite to the railway, and was opened coincidentally with Queensgate.

Westgate, Peterborough.

WESTGATE, 1912

One of the oldest highways in the city, Westgate lead from 'Barnards Cross', near the corner of Long Causeway, to the Spital farm, in which was situated St. Leonards Hospital. This was demolished long ago but leaves its name in Spital Bridge. Double tram lines were laid along Westgate, this tram heading for Queens Drive. On the right at the junction of Queen Street can be seen H. Trollopes & Son, clothiers, built in 1884. Next door is another clothiers store belonging to Walter Riseley, Mayor of the City in 1920.

WESTGATE, 1991

Looking east towards Long Causeway one or two of the older buildings can still be recognised, but the foreground of our picture is dominated by the modern buildings of today. On the left is the Co-operative Society's 'Westgate House', taking its name from a large house that once stood on the corner of Park Road and Westgate. On the right is one of the entrances to the shopping complex of Queensgate, opened in November 1982 by Queen Beatrix of the Netherlands and built over the old Queen Street. Trollopes department store was demolished in the 1970s.

PARK ROAD CO-OPERATIVE STORES, 1912

A detailed view of the Co-op Central Stores; photographed at the beginning of Park Road at its junction with Westgate. This fine building also possessed a dance hall on its first floor. Note the fish cart parked in front of the fishmonger and butchery department. Separate entrances to all departments could be accessed via Park Road. The general store offered everything from a haircut to fancy goods and alcohol.

WESTGATE HOUSE, 1991

The scene today is a little different, with alterations to the exterior at ground level. The clock in this picture was given as a memorial to the fallen in the first world war. It was unveiled, and dedicated to the 31 workers who did not return, by the Lord Bishop of Peterborough (The Right Rev. Theodore Woods, D.D.) before a huge gathering at 2pm on Saturday 29 January 1921.

WESTGATE, PETERBOROUGH.

WESTGATE, 1914

The junction of Park Road and Westgate. Shops on the left include Boots Cash Chemist Ltd.; William Hubbard, basket maker; Henry Barrett, tobacconist; Miss Wheatley's British Infants' School; Cliffe Brothers, glass and china warehousemen; the Bull Commercial Hotel; Kingdon Ellis, surgeon; then Leonard Cane, physician, who lived in the Mansion House. On the far right stand the premises of Thomas Walker, surgeon; A Morfey, confectioner; William Bates, coachman; Wickham & Co., hairdressers; Peter Lowe, fruiterer and florist; Golden Fleece Inn; Charles Foote, cabinet maker; Frederick Metz, pork butcher; etc.

WESTGATE, 1991
Only the Bull Hotel and Barrett's Westgate corner shop remain, along with the premises of 15-19 Westgate; otherwise the view is quite different. One of the entrances to Queensgate is just out of shot on the immediate right. Park Road, on the immediate left, was originally called Houghton Street.

STAR ROAD, 1909

Star Road with the junction of Eastgate on the left. Star Road, formerly Star Lane, ran from Fengate to Padholme Road. On the right, beyond the gaslamp-post is the Durham Ox public house, 76 Star Road, whose proprietor was William Sheffield. On the other corner of Star Road and Glenton Street, opposite the pub, was Bryans Dairy. Beyond the large 7-bedroomed mansion, Rutland House, occupied by Elizabeth Nutt, widow of Thomas Nutt, horse dealer, is a row of one-up and one-down cottages. Thereafter is Nutt Paddock and Stables. Thomas Nutt came to Peterborough in 1873, when our cathedral city was known as a town of 'Pride, Poverty, Parsons and Pubs'.

STAR ROAD, 1991

Peterborough Development Corporation, after demolishing Eastgate, Wellington Street and South Street, and building new council houses and flats, revived the old names but not the old characters and amusing incidents of Boongate, according to the few remaining residents of the Victorian and Edwardian period. Today Nutt's corner looks very flat, with Rutland Court council properties having been built, although the row of terraces on the right remains little changed.

Boongate was also home to the first Italian family; namely that of Mr Joseph Salderini in the mid-nineteenth century.

EASTFIELD ROAD, 1924

Once called Thorney Road, this was a country road to Newark and beyond. It became Eastfield Road in the 1880s. On the left is Padholme Road, which takes its name from a marshy patch of land, home to a large number of toads and subject to flooding. In the centre of our picture is the firm of Dickens & Son, stone, marble and granite monumental sculptors at 81 Eastfield Road; the family name is remembered in Dickens Street. The lovely marble statues standing above the gateposts at 91 Eastfield Road are evidence of the very skilled craft of another monumental mason called Joseph Stephen.

EASTFIELD ROAD, 1991

Now minus the passing loops of the electric tramway and with more commercial properties, this scene is still easily recognisable today. The trees have been removed from the edge of the road, but others take their place behind the cemetery walls. Called the Broadway cemetery, it dates from 1858, and before that the parish burial ground was at the western end of Cowgate. Eastfield Road and the area between St. Mary's Church and Padholme Road used to be generally referred to as Cemetery End. A new cemetery of 58 acres was opened at Newark Hill in 1919.

DOGSTHORPE, early 1900s

Once a village with a population of 500 at the end of the last century, Dogsthorpe is now intergrated into the City of Peterborough. Dogsthorpe Road, previously called Garton End Road, was the main road into the village. The tram terminus was located here for the service that ran from the Market Place. In the background stands the Bluebell Inn, c.1665, with its random-coursed stonework, ashler quoins and collyweston roof, looking exactly the same as the Blue Boar Inn at the nearby village of Eye.

DOGTHORPE, 1991

Now enlarged towards the west and north, the Bluebell Inn still stands in a prominent position at the road junction. The houses on the right and the thatched cottage in the centre still remain, but with the addition of a bus shelter and the City Tyre garage. Dogsthorpe is well known as the home of the City Fire Brigade, with the first ten-bay station built in 1941 and subsequently replaced by a new station and headquarters on the same site in 1964.

Peterborough, Cow Gate.

COWGATE, 1912

Looking down Cowgate towards Cathedral Square, on the corner of King Street can be seen Cornelius Fortune Thomson's large drapery stores known as 'Burlingtons'. There were two sections of this store, each side of King Street, with a connecting footbridge overhead. In 1912 an advert reads, 'These premises are unique, electric passenger lifts to all departments'. On the right can be seen Cash & Co., boot & shoe factors, and Thomas W. Rogers, general warehouseman and toy dealer. The name of the latter's father was perpetuated in Rogers Street, now known as Clarence Road.

COWGATE, 1991

'Burlingtons' store is now replaced by William Brown, estate agents, the modern buildings of Cowgate typifying the present day. Deacon House was situated here with its two adjacent cottages and garden occupying most of the north side of the road, from King Street to the west end of Cowgate. The property was left in Thomas Deacons will of 1721, for the establishment of a charity school for twenty poor boys. In 1878 the school was the recipient of the first telephonic communication carried out in Peterborough from the Drill Hall in Queen Street. The school moved to a site in Deacons Street (formerly called Crown Lane) in 1883 and to its present site in Queens Gardens in 1960.

Cowgate, Peterborough   No. 258

COWGATE, 1957

Here is a splendid view of Cowgate, before Crescent roundabout was constructed, as burgeoning trees are seen centre of the picture. Cowgate runs west of the Cathedral. It existed in 1200, allowing cows to be brought to the abbey gate, now Market Place. The word 'gate' (later becoming street) is from Danelaw and dates back to the tenth and eleventh centuries. In 1721 a toll gate ran across Cowgate, at the foot of where Crescent Bridge now stands.

COWGATE, 1991

The building of Crescent roundabout took place over Peterborough's burial ground, which had existed since 1805. The three acres of farmland at the end of Cowgate was purchased for £540 by St. John The Baptist churchwardens. It began to go out of use by 1859 when the Broadway Cemetery was consecrated. Apart from the building of Crescent roundabout in the early 1970s, little has changed except the ownership and growth of various business premises.

CHURCH STREET AND CORN EXCHANGE, 1953

The Corn Exchange is pictured in the left foreground, with Snowden's Camping and Tent Hire Shop adjacent. By the end of the eighteenth century the Corn Market, one of the busiest in England, was sited just west of St. John's parish church, centre left, and continued to the corner of Queen Street. It was on the site of the Corn Exchange that the city's first theatre and playhouse stood.

CHURCH STREET, 1991

The whole corner site has been redeveloped and Peterborough's General Post Office now occupies the site jointly with Norwich Union Insurance Group. The site of Snowden's shop is partly the premises of Northern Rock Building Society and Norwich Union Insurance Group. Sadly, none of the original shop premises is trading today, as Brown Bros., the butchers, acquired W. & J. Brown, florists and nurserymen's shop, and are of no relation to the original owners.

CUMBERGATE, 1903

Miss Frances Pears, daughter of a Peterborough draper, died in 1901 and left £5000 in her will for new almshouses to be built in Cumbergate. These were completed in 1903. This scene shows the Exchange Street end of Cumbergate, with some of the old buildings, fronting the road being pulled down to make way for a small garden to be built in front of the new almshouses. The house facing us on the left of the picture is now the entrance to the Westgate Arcade, built in 1928-29, and has been preserved and incorporated in the Queensgate Centre.

CUMBERGATE, 1991

Part of the original almshouses, built in 1835, still remains on this corner of Cumbergate, and combined with Miss Pears' almshouses they are now an attractive cafe/bar, keeping the name of this benefactress. The trees are thought to be the original ones planted in this small garden in 1903. Over the years the street of the Woolcombers, as it was known, and this particular corner of it have been the site of a variety of occupants. The Furnus or Common Oven of the town was here, as was the first Moot Hall, demolished in 1615. The House of Correction was demolished in 1844 and the Fire Engine house was moved elsewhere in 1907.

"AEROFILMS SERIES" GENERAL VIEW OF PETERBOROUGH, FROM THE AIR. N° 9851

AERIAL VIEW, mid-1920s

A general view of the city, with Bridge Street and Long Causeway running from the bottom right to top centre. Notice how the skyline is dominated by The Cathedral; St. John's Parish Church; Methodist Church, Wentworth Street; and the Trinity Congregational Church, Priestgate. Other prominent buildings easily identified include Corn Exchange, Church Street; Long Causeway Chambers; Lloyds Bank; Post Office, Cumbergate; and Barford & Perkins Ltd. Engineers, Queen Street. This was prior to their relocation in 1932 to Rochester, Kent, when they amalgamated with Aveling and Porter. The company later moved to Grantham.

AERIAL VIEW, 1991

The centre of the picture shows how Queensgate has completely taken over the landscape. At the top of the picture the Hereward Cross (Arcade) attempts to dwarf The Cathedral. Also the Town Hall has replaced many of the old shops in Narrow Street, which in itself enabled the widening of Bridge Street. The Norwich Union Building now replaces the Corn Exchange next to St. John's Church. The dome of Westgate House can be seen on the corner of Westgate and Park Road, in the top left hand corner.

Local titles published by S.B. Publications in the series: "A Portrait in Old Picture Postcards"

The Soke of Peterborough
Peterborough, Vols. 1, 2 & 3
Huntingdonshire, Vols. 1 & 2
Ted Mott's Cambridge
The Villages of Old Cambridgeshire
Wicken — A Fen Village

Hertfordshire, Vols. 1, 2 & 3

Enfield
From Highgate to Hornsey
The Parish of St. Mary, Islington
Islington and Clerkenwell
Southall

Eastbourne, Vols. 1 & 2
Seaford, Vols. 1 & 2
Brighton & Hove, Vol. 1

Norwich, Vols. 1, 2 & 3
Holt and District
Melton Constable and District
The Norfolk Broads
Thetford and District
Great Yarmouth, Vol. 1
West Norfolk
Diss and District
From Swaffham to Fakenham
Norfolk Railways, Vols. 1 & 2
Herring Heydays

Beccles and Bungay
East Suffolk
Lowestoft, Vol. 1
West Suffolk: Elmswell to Elveden

Other local titles available and in preparation. For full details write (enclosing S.A.E.) to:
S.B. Publications, Unit 2, The Old Station Yard, Pipe Gate, Market Drayton, Shropshire, TF9 4HY.